# UNDERSTANDING THE FEDERAL COURTS

## ADMINISTRATIVE OFFICE OF THE U.S. COURTS

This publication was developed by the Administrative Office of the United
States Courts to provide an introduction to the federal judicial system, its
organization and administration, and its relationship to the legislative and
executive branches of the government. The Administrative Office, the judicial
branch's central support agency, provides a broad range of management,
legal, technical, communications, and other support services for the
administration of the federal courts.

# CONTENTS

# THE CONSTITUTION AND THE FEDERAL JUDICIARY

Article III of the United States Constitution establishes the judicial branch as one of the three separate and distinct branches of the federal government. The other two are the legislative and executive branches.

The federal courts often are called the guardians of the Constitution because their rulings protect rights and liberties guaranteed by the Constitution. Through fair and impartial judgments, the federal courts interpret and apply the law to resolve disputes. The courts do not enact the laws; that is the responsibility of Congress. Nor do the courts have the power to enforce the laws; that is the role of the President and the many executive branch departments and agencies.

The founders of the nation considered an independent federal judiciary essential to ensure fairness and equal justice for all citizens of the United States. The Constitution they drafted promotes judicial independence in two major ways. First, Article III federal judges are appointed for life, and they can be removed from office only through impeachment and conviction by Congress of "Treason, Bribery, or other high Crimes and Misdemeanors." Second, the Constitution provides that the compensation of Article III federal judges "shall not be diminished during their Continuance in Office," which means that neither the President nor Congress can reduce the salary of a federal judge. These two protections help an independent judiciary to decide cases free from popular passion and political influence. ∎

## U.S. CONSTITUTION
## ARTICLE III

The judicial power of the United States shall be vested in one supreme Court, and in such inferior Courts as the Congress may from time to time ordain and establish. The Judges, both of the supreme and inferior Courts, shall hold their Offices during good Behaviour, and shall, at stated Times, receive for their Services, a Compensation, which shall not be diminished during their Continuance in Office.

# THE FEDERAL COURTS IN AMERICAN GOVERNMENT

The three branches of the federal government—legislative, executive, and judicial—operate within a constitutional system of "checks and balances." This means that although each branch is formally separate from the other two, the Constitution often requires cooperation among the branches. Federal laws, for example, are passed by Congress and signed by the President. The judicial branch, in turn, has the authority to decide the constitutionality of federal laws and resolve other disputes over federal laws, but judges depend upon the executive branch to enforce court decisions.

## The Federal Courts and Congress

The Constitution gives Congress the power to create federal courts other than the Supreme Court and to determine their jurisdiction. It is Congress, not the judiciary, that controls the type of cases that may be addressed in the federal courts.

Congress has three other basic responsibilities that determine how the courts will operate. First, it decides how many judges there should be and where they will work. Second, through the confirmation process, Congress determines which of the President's judicial nominees ultimately become federal judges. Third, Congress approves the federal courts' budget and appropriates money for the judiciary to operate. The judiciary's budget is a very small part—two tenths of one percent—of the entire federal budget.

## The Federal Courts and the Executive Branch

Under the Constitution, the President appoints federal judges with the "advice and consent" of the Senate. The President usually consults senators or other elected officials concerning candidates for vacancies on the federal courts.

The President's power to appoint new federal judges is not the judiciary's only interaction with the executive branch. The Department of Justice, which is responsible for prosecuting federal crimes and for representing the government in civil cases, is the most frequent litigator in the federal court system. Several executive branch agencies assist the judiciary with its administrative operations. The United States Marshals Service, for example, provides security for federal courthouses and judges, and the General Services

Administration builds and maintains federal courthouses.

Specialized subject-matter courts and boards, and numerous federal administra-tive agencies adjudicate disputes involving specific federal laws and benefits programs. These non-judiciary courts and tribunals include the United States Tax Court, the United States Court of Appeals for the Armed Forces, and the United States Court of Appeals for Veterans Claims.

While these courts, also known as Article I courts, are not part of the judicial branch, Congress created them to maintain a certain degree of independence and to operate impartially and without political influence. The decisions of these agencies and courts are in some cases appealable to the Article III courts.

## The Federal Courts and the Public

With certain very limited exceptions, each step of the federal judicial process is open to the public. Many federal court-houses are historic buildings, and all are designed to inspire in the public a respect for the tradition and purpose of the American judicial process.

An individual citizen who wishes to observe a court in session may go to the federal courthouse, check the court calen-dar, and watch a proceeding. Anyone may review the pleadings and other documents in a case by going to the clerk of court's office and viewing the appropriate case file using an electronic access terminal. Unlike most state courts, however, the federal courts are just beginning to permit limited live television or radio coverage of some civil trials.

Court dockets and case files also are available on the Internet through the Public Access to Court Electronic Records system (known as "PACER"), at www.pacer.uscourts. gov. In addition, every federal court maintains a website with information about court rules and procedures. A list of these local court websites is available on the judiciary's official website at www.uscourts.gov.

The right of public access to court proceedings is partly derived from the Constitution and partly from court tradi-tion. By conducting their judicial work in public view, judges enhance public confi-dence in the courts and allow citizens to learn first-hand how our judicial system works.

Although there is a very strong presumption that all court records and proceedings are open to the public, public access may be limited in some situations. In a high-profile trial, for example, there may not be enough space in the courtroom to accommodate everyone who would like to observe. Access to the courtroom also may be restricted for security or privacy reasons, such as the protection of a juvenile or a confidential informant. Finally, certain documents may be placed under seal by the judge, meaning that they are not available to the public. Examples of sealed information include confidential business records, certain law enforcement reports, and juvenile records. ∎

# STRUCTURE OF THE FEDERAL COURTS

The Supreme Court is the highest court in the United States. Article III of the U.S. Constitution created the Supreme Court and authorized Congress to pass laws establishing a system of lower courts. In the federal court system's present form, 94 district-level trial courts and 13 courts of appeals sit below the Supreme Court.

## Trial Courts

The U.S. district courts are the primary trial courts of the federal court system. Within limits set by Congress and the Constitution, the district courts have jurisdiction to hear nearly all categories of federal cases, including both civil and criminal matters. There are 94 federal judicial districts, including at least one district in each state, the District of Columbia, and Puerto Rico. Each district includes a U.S. bankruptcy court as a unit of the district court.

There are two special trial courts that have nationwide jurisdiction over certain types of cases. The Court of International Trade addresses cases involving international trade and customs issues. The United States Court of Federal Claims has jurisdiction over most claims for money damages against the United States, disputes over federal contracts, unlawful "takings" of private property by the federal government, vaccine injury cases, and a variety of other claims against the United States.

Three territories of the United States—the Virgin Islands, Guam, and the Northern Mariana Islands—have U.S. district courts that hear federal cases, including bankruptcy cases.

## Appellate Courts

The 94 judicial districts are organized into 12 regional circuits, each of which has a United States court of appeals. A court of appeals hears challenges to district court decisions from courts located within its circuit, as well as appeals from decisions of federal administrative agencies. In addition, the Court of Appeals for the Federal Circuit has nationwide jurisdiction to hear appeals in specialized cases, such as those involving patent laws and cases decided by the Court of International Trade and the Court of Federal Claims.

## United States Supreme Court

The U.S. Supreme Court consists of the Chief Justice of the United States and eight associate justices. At its discretion, and within certain guidelines established by Congress, the Supreme Court hears a small percentage of the cases it is asked to decide each year. Supreme Court cases are usually selected either because the lower courts have differed, or "split," on a legal issue or they involve important questions about the Constitution or federal law. ■

# THE UNITED STATES FEDERAL COURTS

**SUPREME COURT**

**UNITED STATES SUPREME COURT**

**APPELLATE COURTS**

**U.S. COURTS OF APPEALS**
12 Regional Circuit Courts of Appeals
1 U.S. Court of Appeals for the
Federal Circuit

**TRIAL COURTS**

**U.S. DISTRICT COURTS**
94 Judicial Districts and U.S. Bankruptcy Courts
U.S. Court of International Trade
U.S. Court of Federal Claims

**FEDERAL TRIBUNALS AND OTHER ENTITIES**

Military Courts (Trial and Appellate)
Court of Appeals for Veterans Claims
U.S. Tax Court
Federal administrative agencies and boards

# THE JURISDICTION OF THE FEDERAL COURTS

Before a federal court can hear a case, or "exercise its jurisdiction," certain conditions must be met.

First, under the Constitution, federal courts exercise only "judicial" powers. This means that federal judges may interpret the law only through the resolution of actual legal disputes, referred to in Article III of the Constitution as "Cases or Controversies." A court cannot attempt to correct a problem on its own initiative, or to answer a hypothetical legal question.

Second, in an actual case or controversy, the plaintiff in a federal lawsuit also must have legal "standing" to ask the court for a decision. That means the plaintiff must have been aggrieved, or legally harmed in some way, by the defendant.

Third, the case must present a category of dispute that the law in question was designed to address, and it must be a complaint that the court has the power to remedy. In other words, the court must be authorized, under the Constitution or a federal law, to hear the case and grant appropriate relief to the plaintiff.

Finally, the case cannot be "moot," that is, it must present an ongoing problem for the court to resolve. The federal courts, thus, are courts of "limited" jurisdiction because they may only decide certain types of cases as provided by Congress or as identified in the Constitution.

Although the details of the complex web of federal jurisdiction that Congress has given the federal courts is beyond the scope of this brief guide, it is important to understand that there are two main sources of the cases coming before the federal courts: "federal question" jurisdiction and "diversity" jurisdiction.

In general, federal question jurisdiction arises in cases that involve the U.S. government, the U.S. Constitution or federal laws, or controversies between states or between the United States and foreign governments. A case that raises such a "federal question" may be filed in federal court. Examples of such cases might include a claim by an individual for entitlement to money under a federal government program such as Social Security, a criminal prosecution by the government that alleges someone violated a federal law, or a challenge to actions taken by a federal agency.

A case also may be filed in federal court based on the "diversity of citizenship" of the litigants, such as between citizens of different states, or between U.S. citizens and those of another country. To ensure fairness to the out-of-state litigant, the Constitution provides that such cases may be heard in a federal court. An important limit to diversity jurisdiction is that only cases involving more than $75,000 in potential damages may be filed in a federal court. Claims below that amount may only be pursued in state court. Moreover, any diversity jurisdiction case regardless of the amount of money involved may be brought in a state court rather than a federal court.

Federal courts also have jurisdiction over all bankruptcy matters, which Congress has determined should be addressed in federal courts rather than the state courts. Through the bankruptcy process, individuals or businesses that can no longer pay their creditors may either seek a court-supervised liquidation of their assets, or they may reorganize their financial affairs and work out a plan to pay their debts.

Although federal courts are located in every state, they are not the only forum available to potential litigants. In fact, the great majority of legal disputes in American courts, civil or criminal, are addressed in the separate state court systems. State courts have jurisdiction over virtually all divorce and child custody matters, probate and inheritance issues, real estate questions, and juvenile matters, and they handle most criminal cases, contract disputes, traffic violations, and personal injury cases. In addition, certain categories of legal disputes may be resolved in special courts or entities that are part of the federal executive or legislative branches or state and federal administrative agencies. ■

## Geographic Boundaries
### of United States Courts of Appeals and United States District Courts

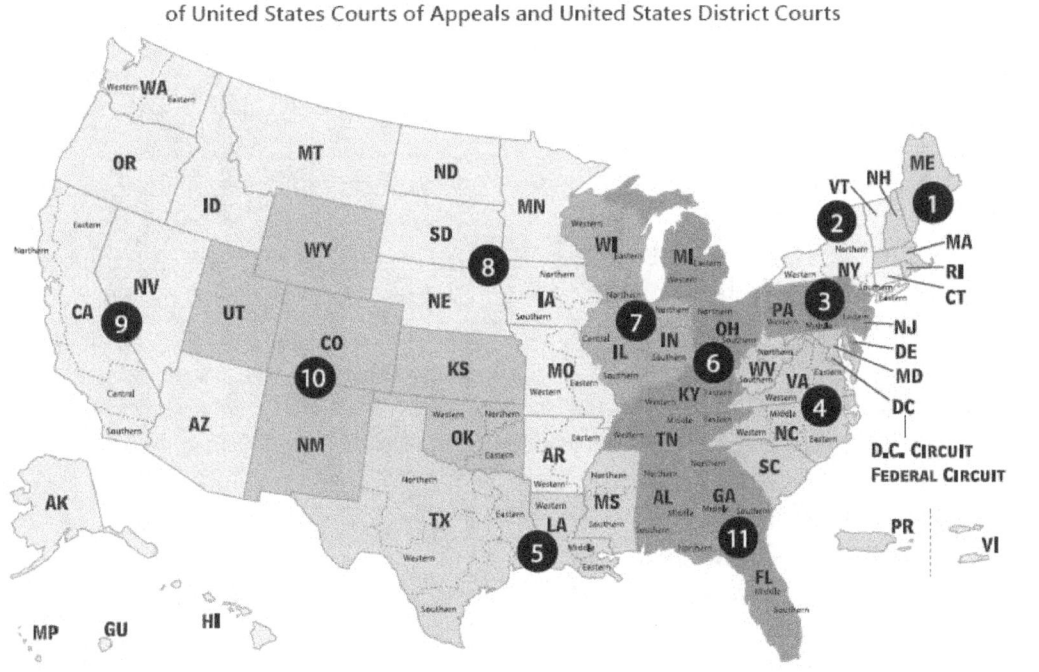

# UNITED STATES JUDGES

The work of the federal courts touches upon many of the most significant issues affecting the American people, and federal judges exercise wide authority and discretion in the cases over which they preside. This section discusses how federal judges are chosen, and provides basic information on judicial compensation, ethics, and the role of senior and recalled judges.

## Appointment and Compensation

Justices of the Supreme Court, judges of the courts of appeals and the district courts, and judges of the Court of International Trade are appointed under Article III of the Constitution by the President of the United States with the advice and consent of the Senate. Article III judges are appointed for life, and they can only be removed from office through the impeachment process. Although there are no special qualifications to become a judge of these courts, those who are nominated are typically very accomplished private or government attorneys, judges in state courts, magistrate judges or bankruptcy judges, or law professors. The judiciary plays no role in the nomination or confirmation process.

Bankruptcy and magistrate judges are judicial officers of district courts. The President and Senate have no role in their selection. Congress determines the number and location of bankruptcy judges; they are appointed by the courts of appeals. The district court determines the number and location of magistrate judges and appoints them. Judges of the Court of Federal Claims are appointed by the President with the advice and consent of the Senate.

Each court in the federal system has a chief judge who, in addition to hearing cases, has administrative responsibilities relating to the operation of the court. The chief judge is normally the judge who has served on the court the longest. Chief district and court of appeals judges must be under age 65 to be designated as chief judge. They may serve for a maximum of seven years and may not serve as chief judge beyond the age of 70.

All federal judges receive salaries and benefits that are set by Congress.

## CODE OF CONDUCT FOR UNITED STATES JUDGES

A judge should uphold the integrity and independence of the judiciary.

A judge should avoid impropriety and the appearance of impropriety in all activities.

A judge should perform the duties of the office fairly, impartially, and diligently.

A judge may engage in extrajudicial activities that are consistent with the obligations of judicial office.

A judge should refrain from political activity.

### Judicial Ethics

Federal judges abide by the Code of Conduct for United States Judges, a set of ethical principles and guidelines adopted by the Judicial Conference of the United States. The Code of Conduct provides guidance for judges on issues of judicial integrity and independence, judicial diligence and impartiality, permissible extra-judicial activities, and the avoidance of impropriety or even its appearance.

Judges may not hear cases in which they have personal knowledge of the disputed facts, a personal bias concerning a party to the case, earlier involvement in the case as a lawyer, or a financial interest in any party or subject matter of the case.

Many federal judges devote time to public service and educational activities. They have a distinguished history of service to the legal profession through their writing, speaking, and teaching. This important role is recognized in the Code of Conduct, which encourages judges to engage in activities to improve the law, the legal system, and the administration of justice.

### Senior and Recalled Judges

Court of appeals, district court, and Court of International Trade judges have life tenure, and they may retire if they are at least 65 years old and meet certain years of service requirements. Most Article III judges who are eligible to retire decide to continue to hear cases on a full-time or part-time basis as "senior judges." Retired bankruptcy, magistrate, and Court of Federal Claims judges also may be "recalled" to active service. Without the efforts of senior and recalled judges, the judiciary would need many more judges to handle its cases. ∎

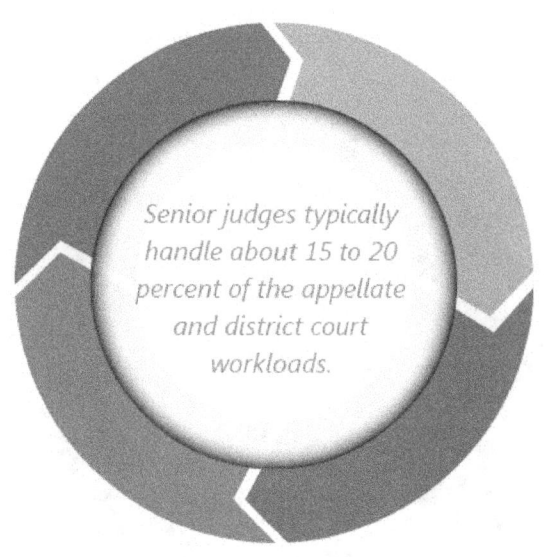

Senior judges typically handle about 15 to 20 percent of the appellate and district court workloads.

# THE FEDERAL JUDICIAL PROCESS IN BRIEF

This section describes three key features of the federal judicial system and gives an overview of the process in criminal cases, civil cases, and bankruptcy proceedings. Also included are brief descriptions of jury service and selection procedures and the appeals process.

## An Adversarial System

The litigation process in U.S. courts is referred to as an "adversarial" system because it relies on the litigants to present their dispute before a neutral fact-finder. According to American legal tradition, inherited from the English common law, the clash of adversaries before the court is most likely to allow the jury or judge to determine the truth and resolve the dispute at hand. In some other legal systems, judges or other court officials investigate and assist the parties to find relevant evidence or obtain testimony from witnesses. In the United States, the work of collecting evidence and preparing to present it to the court is accomplished by the litigants and their attorneys, normally without assistance from the court.

*To avoid the expense and delay of having a trial, judges encourage the litigants to try to reach an agreement resolving their dispute...*

## Fees and the Costs of Litigation

Another characteristic of the American judicial system is that litigants typically pay their own court and attorneys' fees whether they win or lose. Most court fees are set by Congress. Other costs of litigation, such as attorneys and experts fees, are more substantial. In criminal cases, the government pays the costs of investigation and prosecution. The court also provides a lawyer without cost for any criminal defendant who is unable to afford one. In civil cases, plaintiffs who cannot afford to pay court fees may seek permission from the court to proceed without paying those fees.

## Procedural Rules for Conducting Litigation

There are federal rules of evidence and procedural rules governing civil, criminal, bankruptcy, and appellate cases that must be followed in the federal courts. The rules are designed to promote simplicity, fairness, the just determination of litigation, and the elimination of unjustifiable expense and delay. Committees of judges, lawyers, and professors appointed by the Chief Justice draft the rules. The Administrative Office publishes the rules for public comment. Rules are approved by the Judicial Conference of the United States, and promulgated by the Supreme Court. The rules become law unless the Congress votes to reject or modify them.

## Civil Cases

A federal civil case involves a legal dispute between two or more parties. To begin a civil lawsuit in federal court, the plaintiff files a complaint with the court and "serves" a copy of the complaint on the defendant. The complaint describes the plaintiff's damages or injury, explains how the defendant caused the harm, shows that the court has jurisdiction, and asks the court to order relief. A plaintiff may seek money to compensate for the damages, or may ask the court to order the defendant to stop the conduct that is causing the harm. The court may also order other types of relief, such as a declaration of the legal rights of the plaintiff in a particular situation.

To prepare a case for trial, the litigants may conduct "discovery." In discovery, the litigants must provide information to each other about the case, such as the identity of witnesses and copies of any documents related to the case. The purpose of discovery is to prepare for trial by requiring the litigants to assemble their evidence and prepare to call witnesses. Each side also may file requests, or "motions," with the court seeking rulings on the discovery of evidence, or on the procedures to be followed at trial.

One common method of discovery is the deposition. In a deposition a witness is required to answer questions about the case before the trial. Lawyers "depose" the witness by asking questions that the witness answers, under oath, in the presence of a court reporter. The court reporter is a person specially trained to record all testimony and produce a word-for-word account called a transcript.

To avoid the expense and delay of having a trial, judges encourage the litigants to try to reach an agreement resolving their dispute. In particular, the courts encourage the use of mediation, arbitration, and other forms of alternative dispute resolution, or "ADR," designed to produce an early resolution of a dispute without the need for trial or other court proceedings. As a result, litigants often decide to resolve a civil lawsuit with an agreement known as a "settlement."

If a case is not settled, the court will schedule a trial. In a wide variety of civil cases, either side is entitled under the Constitution to request a jury trial. If the parties waive their right to a jury, then the case will be heard by a judge without a jury.

At a trial, witnesses testify under the supervision of a judge. By applying rules of evidence, the judge determines which information may be presented in the courtroom. To ensure that witnesses speak from their own knowledge and do not change their story based on what they hear another witness say, witnesses are kept out of the courtroom until it is time for them to testify. A court reporter keeps a record of the trial proceedings. A deputy clerk of court also keeps a record of each person who testifies and marks for the record any documents, photographs, or other items introduced into evidence.

As the questioning of a witness proceeds, the opposing attorney may object to a question if it invites the witness to say something that is not based on the witness's personal knowledge, is unfairly prejudicial, or is irrelevant to the case. The judge rules on the objection, generally by ruling that it is either sustained or overruled. If the objection is sustained, the witness does not answer the question, and the attorney must move on to his next question. The court reporter records the objections so that a court of appeals can review the arguments later if necessary.

At the conclusion of the evidence, each side gives a closing argument. In a jury trial, the judge will explain the law that is relevant to the case and the decisions the jury needs to make. The jury generally is asked to determine whether the defendant is responsible for harming the plaintiff in some way, and then to determine the amount of damages that the defendant will be required to pay. If the case is being tried before a judge without a jury, known as a "bench" trial, the judge will decide these

*The standard of proof in a criminal trial is proof "beyond a reaonable doubt," which means the evidence must be so strong that there is no reasonable doubt that the defendant committed the crime.*

issues or order some kind of relief to the prevailing party. In a civil case the plaintiff must convince the jury by a "preponderance of the evidence" (i.e., that it is more likely than not) that the defendant is responsible for the harm the plaintiff has suffered.

## Criminal Cases

The judicial process in a criminal case differs from a civil case in several important ways. At the beginning of a federal criminal case, the principal actors are the U.S. attorney (the prosecutor) and the grand jury. The U.S. attorney represents the United States in most court proceedings, including all criminal prosecutions. The grand jury reviews evidence presented by the U.S. attorney and decides whether there is sufficient evidence to require a defendant to stand trial.

After a person is arrested, a pretrial services or probation officer of the court immediately interviews the defendant and conducts an investigation of the defendant's background. The information obtained by the pretrial services or probation office will be used to help a judge decide whether to release the defendant into the community before trial, and whether to impose conditions of release. A person accused of a crime is entitled to release before trial, unless the judge determines that the person is likely to be a danger to some other person or the community, is likely to engage in further criminal activity if released, or is not likely to appear for trial.

At an initial appearance, a judge advises the defendant of the charges filed, considers whether the defendant should be held in jail until trial, and determines whether there is probable cause to believe that an offense has been committed and that the defendant has committed it. Defendants who are unable to afford counsel are advised of their right to a court-appointed attorney. The court may appoint either a federal defender or a private attorney who has agreed to accept such appointments from the court. In either type of appointment, the attorney will be paid by the court from funds appropriated by Congress.

Defendants released into the community before trial may be subject to certain restrictions, such as electronic monitoring or drug testing, and required to make periodic reports to a pretrial services officer to ensure appearance at trial.

The defendant enters a plea to the charges brought by the U.S. attorney at a court hearing known as an arraignment. Most defendants—more than 90%—plead guilty rather than go to trial. If a defendant pleads guilty in return for the government agreeing to drop certain charges or to recommend a lenient sentence, the agreement often is called a "plea bargain." If the defendant pleads guilty, the judge may impose a sentence at that time, but more commonly will schedule a hearing to determine the sentence at a later date. In most felony cases the judge waits for the results of a presentence report, prepared by the court's probation office, before imposing a sentence. If the defendant pleads not guilty, the judge will proceed to schedule a trial.

Criminal cases include limited pretrial discovery proceedings, similar to those in civil cases, but with restrictions to protect the identity of government informants and to prevent intimidation of witnesses. The attorneys also may file motions, which are requests for rulings by the court before the trial. For example, defense attorneys often file a motion to suppress evidence, which asks the court to exclude from the trial evidence that the defendant believes was obtained by the government in violation of the defendant's constitutional rights.

In a criminal trial, the burden of proof is on the government. Defendants do not have to prove their innocence. Instead, the government must provide evidence to convince the jury of the defendant's guilt. The standard of proof in a criminal trial gives the prosecutor a much greater burden than the plaintiff in a civil trial. The defendant must be found guilty "beyond a reasonable doubt," which means the evidence must be so strong that there is no reasonable doubt that the defendant committed the crime.

If a defendant is found not guilty, the defendant is released and the government may not appeal. The person may not be charged again for the same offense in a federal court. The Constitution prohibits "double jeopardy," or being tried twice for the same offense.

If the verdict is guilty, the judge determines the defendant's sentence. The United States Sentencing Commission issues federal sentencing guidelines which are advisory, but judges must still consider them when determining a defendant's sentence. The court's probation office prepares a report for the court that considers the individual defendant and the crimes for which he or she has been found guilty. During sentencing, the court may consider not only the recommendation in the sentencing guidelines and the evidence produced at trial, but also relevant information that may be provided by the pretrial services officer, the U.S. attorney, and the defense attorney.

A sentence may include time in prison, a fine to be paid to the government, and restitution to be paid to crime victims. The court's probation officers assist the court in enforcing any conditions that are imposed as part of a criminal sentence. The supervision of offenders also may involve services such as substance abuse testing and treatment programs, job counseling, and alternative detention options, such as home confinement or electronic monitoring.

## Jury Service

One of the most important ways individual citizens become involved with the federal judicial process is by serving as jurors. There are two types of juries serving distinct functions in the federal trial courts: trial juries (also known as petit juries), and grand juries.

The functioning of a trial jury varies slightly depending upon whether the trial is for a civil or criminal case. A civil trial jury typically consists of 6 to 12 persons, while a criminal trial jury is made up of 12 jurors. In a civil case, the role of the jury is to listen to the evidence presented, to decide whether the defendant injured the plaintiff or otherwise failed to fulfill a legal duty to the plaintiff, and to determine what the remedy, compensation, or penalty should be. Criminal juries decide whether the defendant committed the crime as charged, while a judge determines the defendant's sentence. Verdicts in both civil and criminal cases must be unanimous, unless the parties in a civil case agree to a non-unanimous verdict. A jury's deliberations are conducted in private, out of sight and hearing of the judge, litigants, witnesses, and others in the courtroom.

A grand jury, which consists of 16 to 23 members, has a specialized function to perform before a felony criminal case is filed in the district court. The U.S. attorney, the prosecutor in federal criminal cases, presents evidence to the grand jury for them to determine whether there is "probable cause" to believe that an individual has committed a crime and should be put on trial. If the grand jury decides there is enough

## JUROR QUALIFICATIONS AND EXEMPTIONS

### Qualifications to be a Juror

United States citizen

At least 18 years of age

Reside in the judicial district for one year

Adequate proficiency in English

No disqualifying mental or physical condition

Not currently subject to felony charges

Never convicted of a felony (unless civil rights have been legally restored)

### Exemptions from Service

Active duty members of the armed forces

Members of police and fire departments

Certain public officials

Others based on individual court rules (such as members of voluntary emergency service organizations and people who recently have served on a jury)

### Temporary Deferrals of Service

May be granted at the court's discretion on the grounds of "undue hardship or extreme inconvenience."

evidence, it will issue an indictment against the defendant. Grand jury proceedings are not open for public observation.

## Jury Selection Procedures

Potential jurors are selected from any source that will yield a representative sample of the judicial district's population. Most often, jurors are chosen from a pool generated by a random selection of citizens' names from lists of registered voters, or combined lists of voters and people with a driver's license. The potential jurors complete questionnaires to help determine whether they are qualified to serve on a jury. After reviewing the questionnaires, the court randomly selects individuals to be summoned to appear for jury duty. These selection methods help ensure that jurors represent a cross section of the community, without regard to race, gender, national origin, age, or political affiliation. Jurors receive modest compensation and expenses from the court for their service.

Being summoned for jury service does not guarantee that an individual actually will serve on a jury. When a jury is needed for a trial, the group of qualified jurors is taken to the courtroom where the trial will take place. The judge and the attorneys then ask the potential jurors questions to determine their suitability to serve on the jury, a process called voir dire. The purpose of voir dire is to exclude from the jury people who may not be able to decide the case fairly. Members of the panel who know any person involved in the case, who have information about the

case, or who may have strong prejudices about the people or issues involved in the case typically will be excused by the judge. The attorneys also may exclude a limited number of jurors without giving a reason.

## TERMS OF JURY SERVICE

### Length of Service

Trial jury service varies by court.

Some courts require service for one day or for the duration of one trial; others require service for a fixed term of up to one month (or more if a trial is longer).

Grand jury service may last up to 24 months.

### Payment

$40 per day; in some instances jurors may also receive meal and travel allowances.

### Employment Protections

By law, employers must allow employees time off  (paid or unpaid) for jury service. The law also forbids any employer from firing, intimidating, or coercing any permanent employee because of their federal jury service.

## Bankruptcy Cases

Federal courts have exclusive jurisdiction over bankruptcy cases. This means a bankruptcy case may not be filed in a state court.

The primary purposes of the law of bankruptcy are:

❶ to give an honest debtor a "fresh start" in life by relieving the debtor of most debts;

❷ to repay creditors in a fair and orderly manner to the extent that the debtor has property available for payment;

❸ to reorganize a failing business by restructuring debt or the business entity itself, or, alternatively, to provide a framework for the orderly liquidation of the failed enterprise; and

❹ to deter and remedy dishonest actions by debtors or creditors that would have the effect of undermining the purposes of bankruptcy law.

A bankruptcy case normally begins by the debtor filing a petition with the bankruptcy court. A petition may be filed by an individual, by a husband and wife together, or by a corporation or other entity. The debtor is also required to file statements listing assets, income, liabilities, and the names and addresses of all creditors and how much they are owed. The filing of the petition automatically prevents, or "stays," debt collection actions against the debtor and the debtor's property. As long as the stay remains in effect, creditors cannot bring or continue lawsuits, make wage garnishments, or even make telephone calls demanding payment. Creditors receive notice from the clerk of court that the debtor has filed a bankruptcy petition.

Some bankruptcy cases are filed to allow a debtor to reorganize and establish a plan to repay creditors, while other cases involve liquidation of the debtor's property. In many bankruptcy cases involving liquidation of the property of individual consumers, there is little or no money available from the debtor's estate to pay creditors. As a result, in these cases there are few issues or disputes, and the debtor is normally granted a "discharge" of most debts without objection. This means that the debtor will no longer be personally liable for repaying the debts.

In other cases, however, disputes may give rise to litigation in a bankruptcy case over such matters as who owns certain property, how it should be used, what the property is worth, how much is owed on a debt, whether the debtor should be discharged from certain debts, or how

# CATEGORIES OF BANKRUPTCY CASES

## Chapter 7 (Liquidation)

Chapter 7 is designed to repay debts owed to creditors by selling most of the debtor's property. When a Chapter 7 case is filed, a trustee is appointed to take over the debtor's property for the benefit of the debtor's creditors. The debtor, however, is allowed to keep a limited amount of "exempt" property specified by law. The trustee then sells all non-exempt property of the debtor and distributes the proceeds to creditors in accordance with procedures set forth in the bankruptcy laws.

## Chapter 13 (Debt Adjustment of an Individual)

In a Chapter 13 bankruptcy, the debtor may keep his or her property, but must repay creditors in installments taken from the debtor's future earnings. A debtor is required to submit a plan for approval by the court specifying how and when the debts will be repaid to creditors. A trustee is appointed in a Chapter 13 case, and a portion of the debtor's future income, in most cases, is paid to the trustee, who then pays creditors.

## Chapter 11 (Reorganization)

Chapter 11 is designed mainly to give an ongoing business an opportunity to resolve financial problems through reorganization. A trustee is not normally appointed. The debtor is allowed to continue to operate the business under court supervision.

## Chapter 12 (Debt Adjustment of a Family Farmer)

Chapter 12 is similar in many respects to Chapter 13, except that it is available only to family farmers.

## Chapter 9 (Debt Adjustment of a Municipality)

Chapter 9 is available only to a political subdivision (i.e., a city, town, or county), public agency, or other instrumentality of a state.

## Chapter 15 (Cross-Border Insolvency)

Chapter 15 of the Bankruptcy Code authorizes the commencement of a U.S. bankruptcy case related to a foreign case.

much money should be paid to lawyers, accountants, auctioneers, or other professionals. Litigation in the bankruptcy court is conducted in much the same way that civil cases are handled in the district court. There may be discovery, pretrial proceedings, settlement efforts, and a trial.

## The Appeals Process

The losing party in a decision by a trial court in the federal system normally is entitled to appeal the decision to a federal court of appeals. Similarly, a litigant who is not satisfied with a decision made by a federal administrative agency usually may file a petition for review of the agency decision by a court of appeals. Judicial review in cases involving certain federal agencies or programs—for example, disputes over Social Security benefits—may be obtained first in a district court rather than a court of appeals.

In a civil case, either side may appeal the verdict. In a criminal case, the defendant may appeal a guilty verdict, but the government may not appeal if a defendant is found not guilty. Either side in a criminal case may appeal with respect to the sentence that is imposed after a guilty verdict.

In most bankruptcy courts, an appeal of a ruling by a bankruptcy judge may be taken to the district court. Several courts of appeals, however, have established Bankruptcy Appellate Panels consisting of three bankruptcy

*In a criminal case the defendant may appeal a guilty verdict, but the government may not appeal if a defendant is found not guilty.*

judges to hear appeals directly from the bankruptcy courts. In either situation, the party that loses in the initial bankruptcy appeal may then appeal to the court of appeals. Under certain limited circumstances, an appeal may be taken from a ruling by a bankruptcy judge directly to the court of appeals.

A litigant who files an appeal, known as an "appellant," must show that the trial

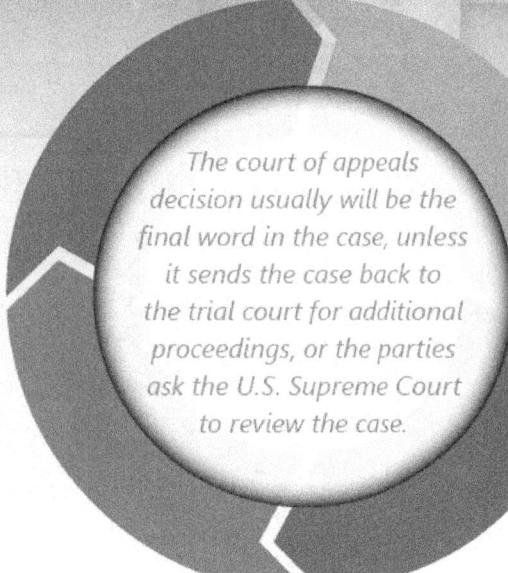

*The court of appeals decision usually will be the final word in the case, unless it sends the case back to the trial court for additional proceedings, or the parties ask the U.S. Supreme Court to review the case.*

court or administrative agency made a legal error that affected the decision in the case. The court of appeals makes its decision based on the record of the case established by the trial court or agency; it does not receive additional evidence or hear witnesses. The court of appeals also may review the factual findings of the trial court or agency, but typically may only overturn a decision on factual grounds if the findings were "clearly erroneous."

Appeals are decided by panels of three judges working together. The appellant presents legal arguments to the panel, in writing, in a document called a "brief." In the brief the appellant tries to persuade the judges that the trial court made an error and that its decision should be reversed. On the other hand, the party defending against the appeal, known as the "appellee," tries in its brief to show why the trial court decision was correct, or why any error made by the trial court was not

significant enough to affect the outcome of the case.

Although some cases are decided on the basis of written briefs alone, many cases are selected for an "oral argument" before the court. Oral argument in the court of appeals is a structured discussion between the appellate lawyers and the panel of judges focusing on the legal principles in dispute. Each side is given a short time—usually about 15 minutes—to present arguments to the court.

The court of appeals decision usually will be the final word in the case, unless it sends the case back to the trial court for additional proceedings, or the parties ask the U.S. Supreme Court to review the case. In some cases the decision may be reviewed en banc, that is, by a larger group of judges (usually all) of the court of appeals.

A litigant who loses in a federal court of appeals, or in the highest court of a state, may file a petition for a "writ of certiorari," which is a document asking the Supreme Court to review the case. The Supreme Court, however, does not have to grant review. The Court typically will agree to hear a case only when it involves an unusually important legal principle, or when two or more federal appellate courts have interpreted a law differently. There are also a small number of special circumstances in which the Supreme Court is required by law to hear an appeal. When the Supreme Court hears a case, the parties are required to file written briefs and the Court may hear oral argument. ∎

# FEDERAL JUDICIAL ADMINISTRATION

## Individual Courts

The day-to-day responsibility for judicial administration rests with each individual court. Each court is given responsibility by statute and administrative practice to appoint support staff, supervise spending, and manage the court's records.

The chief judge of each court plays a key leadership role in overseeing and coordinating the efficient operations of the court. Although the chief judge is generally responsible for overseeing day-to-day court administration, important policy decisions are made by the judges of the court working together.

The clerk of court is the executive hired by the judges of the court to carry out the court's administrative functions. The clerk manages the court's non-judicial functions in accordance with policies set by the court, and reports directly to the court through its chief judge. Among the clerk's many functions are:

- Maintaining the records and dockets of the court
- Managing the court's information technology systems
- Paying all fees, fines, costs, and other monies collected into the U.S. Treasury
- Administering the court's jury system
- Providing interpreters and court reporters
- Sending official court notices and summons
- Providing courtroom support services

## The Circuit Judicial Councils

At the regional level, a "circuit judicial council" in each geographic circuit oversees the administration of the courts located in that circuit. Each circuit judicial council consists of the chief circuit judge, who serves as the chair, and an equal number of other circuit and district judges.

The judicial council oversees numerous aspects of court of appeals and district court operations. The council is given broad authority with a statutory authorization to issue orders to promote accountability and the "effective and expeditious administration of justice within its circuit." Aside from its fundamental responsibility to ensure that individual courts are operating effectively, the judicial council is responsible for reviewing local court rules for consistency with national rules of procedure, approving district court plans on topics such as equal employment opportunity and jury selection, and reviewing complaints of judicial misconduct. Each judicial council appoints a "circuit executive," who works closely with the chief circuit judge to coordinate a wide range of administrative matters in the circuit. ∎

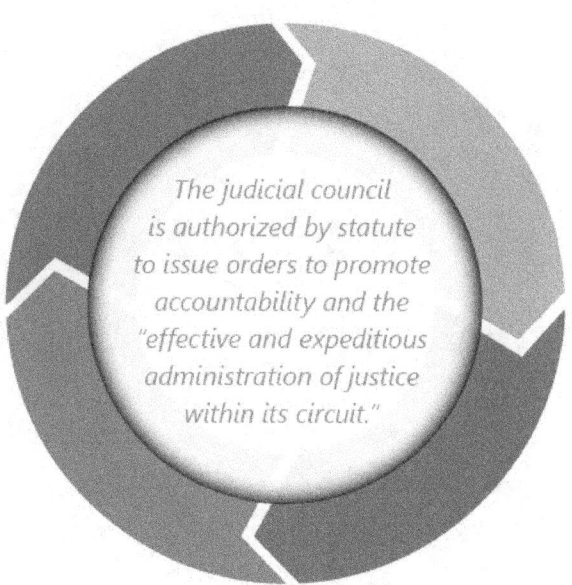

*The judicial council is authorized by statute to issue orders to promote accountability and the "effective and expeditious administration of justice within its circuit."*

# Court Support Staff

In addition to their personal chambers staff of law clerks and secretaries, judges rely on central court support staff to assist in the work of the court. These staff include:

## Clerk

The chief administrative officer of the court, who keeps court records, handles court monies, and supervises court operations.

## Circuit Executive

Performs a broad range of administrative tasks under the direction of the regional circuit judicial council.

## Court Reporters

Make a word-for-word record of court proceedings and prepares a transcript.

## Court Librarian

Maintains court libraries and assists in meeting the information needs of the judges and lawyers.

## Staff Attorneys and Pro Se Law Clerks

Assist the court with research and drafting of opinions.

## Pretrial Services Officers and Probation Officers

Interview defendants before trial, investigate their backgrounds, file reports to assist judges in deciding on pretrial release or sentencing of convicted defendants, and supervise released defendants.

# THE JUDICIAL CONFERENCE OF THE UNITED STATES AND NATIONAL ADMINISTRATION

## The Judicial Conference of the United States

The Judicial Conference of the United States is the federal courts' national policy-making body. The Chief Justice of the United States presides over the Judicial Conference, which consists of 26 other members including the chief judge of each court of appeals, one district court judge from each regional circuit, and the chief judge of the Court of International Trade. The Judicial Conference works through committees established along subject matter lines to recommend national policies and legislation on all aspects of federal judicial administration. Committees include budget, rules of practice and procedure, court administration and case management, criminal law, bankruptcy, judicial resources (judgeships and personnel matters), information technology, and codes of conduct.

## The Administrative Office of the United States Courts

The Administrative Office, an agency within the judicial branch, provides a broad range of legislative, legal, financial, technology, management, administrative, and program support services to the federal courts. The Administrative Office is responsible for carrying out the policies of the Judicial Conference of the United States. A primary responsibility of the Administrative Office is to provide staff support and counsel to the Judicial Conference and its committees. The numerous additional responsibilities of the Administrative Office include collecting and reporting judicial branch statistics, developing budgets, conducting studies and assessments of judiciary operations and programs, providing technical assistance to the courts, developing training programs, and fostering communications within the judiciary and with other branches of government and the public.

The Director of the Administrative Office, who is appointed by the Chief Justice in consultation with the Judicial Conference, serves as the chief administrative officer of the federal courts. Congress vested many of the judiciary's administrative responsibilities in the Director. Recognizing, however, that the courts can make better business decisions based on local needs, the Director delegates the responsibility for many administrative matters to the individual courts. This concept, known as "decentralization," allows each court to operate with considerable autonomy in accordance with policies and guidelines set at the regional and national level.

## The Federal Judicial Center (FJC)

The Federal Judicial Center provides training and research for the federal judiciary in a wide range of areas including court administration, case management, budget and finance, human resources, and court technology. The FJC develops orientation and continuing education programs for judges and other court personnel, including seminars; curriculum materials for use by individual courts; monographs and manuals; and audio, video, and interactive media programs. The FJC conducts studies of judiciary operations, and makes recommendations to the Judicial Conference for improvement of the administration and management of the federal courts. The FJC's operations are overseen by a board of directors consisting of the Chief Justice, the Director of the Administrative Office, and seven judges chosen by the Judicial Conference.

## Judicial Panel for Multidistrict Litigation

The Judicial Panel for Multidistrict Litigation has the authority to transfer cases that are pending in different districts but involve common questions of fact (for example, mass tort actions arising from airplane crashes, breast implants, or asbestos) to a single district for coordinated or consolidated pretrial proceedings. The Panel consists of seven court of appeals and district court judges designated by the Chief Justice.

## United States Sentencing Commission

The United States Sentencing Commission establishes sentencing guidelines for the federal criminal justice system. The Commission also monitors the performance of probation officers with regard to sentencing recommendations, and has established a research program that includes a clearinghouse and information center on federal sentencing practices. The Sentencing Commission consists of a chairman, three vice chairs, and three other voting commissioners who are appointed for six-year terms by the President. ■

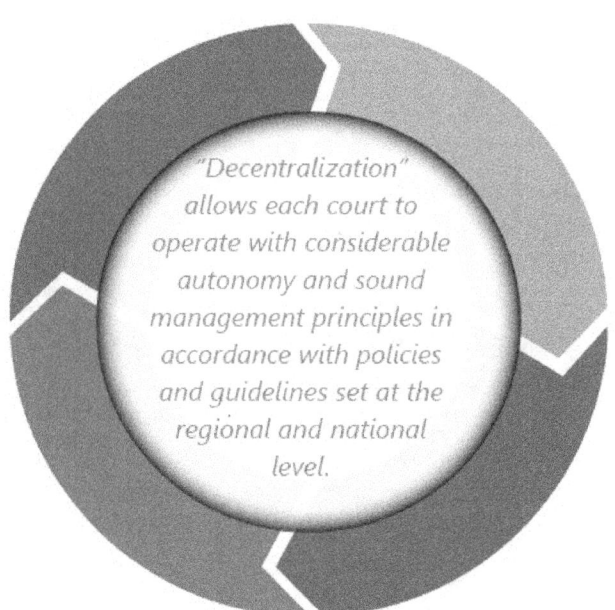

*"Decentralization" allows each court to operate with considerable autonomy and sound management principles in accordance with policies and guidelines set at the regional and national level.*

# THE JUDICIARY'S BUDGET

In recognition of the constitutional separation of powers among the three branches of the federal government, Congress has given the judiciary authority to prepare and execute its own budget. The Administrative Office, in consultation with the courts and with various Judicial Conference committees, prepares a proposed budget for the judiciary each fiscal year. The proposal is reviewed and approved by the Judicial Conference with an accompanying set of detailed justifications. By law, the President must include the judiciary's proposed budget as a part of the unified federal budget submitted to Congress each year. The President may comment on the judiciary's budget request, but the proposal must be transmitted to Congress without change. The congressional appropriations committees conduct hearings at which judges and the Director of the Administrative Office frequently present and justify the judiciary's projected expenditures.

After Congress enacts a budget for the judiciary, the Judicial Conference approves a plan to spend the money and the Administrative Office distributes funds directly to each court, operating unit, and program in the judiciary. Individual courts have considerable authority and flexibility to conduct their work, establish budget priorities, make sound business decisions, hire staff, and make purchases, consistent with Judicial Conference policies. ■

# COMMONLY ASKED QUESTIONS ABOUT THE FEDERAL JUDICIAL PROCESS

## How do I file a civil case? Is there a charge?

A civil action begins when some party to a dispute files a complaint. The parties beginning a civil action in a district court are required to pay a filing fee that is set by statute. A plaintiff who is unable to pay the fee may file a request to proceed in forma pauperis. If the request is granted, the fee is waived.

## How do I file a criminal case?

Individuals may not file criminal charges in federal courts. A criminal proceeding is initiated by the government, usually through the U.S. attorney's office in coordination with a law enforcement agency. Allegations of criminal behavior should be brought to the local police, the FBI, or another appropriate law enforcement agency.

## How do I file for bankruptcy protection? Is there a charge?

A bankruptcy case begins with the filing of a petition. The required forms are available from the bankruptcy court clerk's office, on the court's website, or at many stationery stores. There is a range of filing fees for bankruptcy cases, depending on the chapter of the bankruptcy code under which the case is filed. Chapter 7, the most common type filed by individuals, involves an almost complete liquidation of the assets of the debtor, as well as a discharge of most debts.

## How can I find a lawyer?

Local bar associations usually offer lawyer referral services, often without charge. The clerk's office in each district court usually is able to help find a referral service. But personnel in the clerk's office and other federal court employees are prohibited from providing legal advice to individual litigants.

Defendants in criminal proceedings have a right to a lawyer, and they are entitled to have counsel appointed at government expense if they are financially unable to obtain adequate representation by private counsel. The Criminal Justice Act requires a court determination that a person is financially eligible for court-appointed counsel. Defendants may be required to pay some of these costs. Defendants also have the option of waiving their right to counsel; however, this requires consent of the presiding judge.

There is no general right to free legal assistance in civil proceedings. Some litigants obtain free or low-cost representation through local bar association referrals or legal services organizations. Litigants in civil cases may also proceed pro se; that is, they may represent themselves without the assistance of a lawyer.

## How are judges assigned to a particular court?

Each federal judge is commissioned to a specific court. Judges have no authority to hear cases in other courts unless they are formally designated to do so. Because of heavy caseloads in certain districts, judges from other courts are often asked to hear cases in these districts.

### How are judges assigned to specific cases?

Judge assignment methods vary, but all courts use some random case assignment procedure and manage caseloads so that each judge in a court receives roughly an equal caseload.

### What is a U.S. Magistrate Judge?

Magistrate judges are judicial officers appointed by the district court to serve for eight-year terms. Their duties fall into four general categories: conducting most initial proceedings in criminal cases (including search and arrest warrants, detention hearings, probable cause hearings, and appointment of attorneys); conducting a wide variety of other proceedings in civil and criminal cases as referred to them by district judges (including deciding motions, reviewing petitions filed by prisoners, and conducting pretrial and settlement conferences); trial of most criminal misdemeanor cases; and trial of civil cases with the consent of the parties.

### How can I check on the status of a case?

The clerk's office responds without charge to most inquiries on the status of a case. There is a fee to conduct certain searches and retrieve some information, and to print court documents. Most federal courts have automated systems that allow for the search and retrieval of case-related information at the public counters in the courthouse, and electronically from other locations. In the Supreme Court and many bankruptcy courts, telephone information systems enable callers to obtain case information by touch-tone phone. Court dockets and opinions are also available on the Internet. The judiciary's Internet homepage, www.uscourts.gov, includes links to individual court websites, as well as a directory of court electronic public access services.

## How quickly does a court reach a decision in a particular case?

All cases are handled as expeditiously as possible. The Speedy Trial Act of 1974 establishes special time requirements for the prosecution and disposition of criminal cases in district courts. As a result, courts must give the scheduling of criminal cases a higher priority than civil cases. The Act normally allows only 70 days from a defendant's arrest to the beginning of the trial.

There is no similar law governing civil trial scheduling, but the courts usually are able to resolve civil cases in less than a year. Depending on its complexity, a particular case may require more or less time to resolve. There are many reasons why the progress of a particular case may be delayed, many of which are outside the court's control. Cases may be delayed because settlement negotiations are in progress, or because the attorneys or judge have scheduling conflicts.

## How is staff hired in the federal courts?

The federal court system's personnel decisions are decentralized. This means that each court conducts its own advertising and hiring for job positions. Judges select and hire their own chambers staff. The clerk of court and certain other central court staff are hired by the court as a whole. Other court staff are hired by the clerk of court, who acts under the supervision of the court. Some employment opportunities are listed on the judiciary's Internet homepage, www.uscourts.gov, but often the clerk's office or the website of a particular court is the best source for a complete listing. ∎

# COMMON LEGAL TERMS

### acquittal
Judgment that a criminal defendant has not been proven guilty beyond a reasonable doubt. In other words, a verdict of "not guilty." Under the Double Jeopardy clause of the Constitution, an acquitted defendant may never be tried again criminally for the same offense.

### administrative law judge
An officer in a regulatory or social service agency, such as the Securities and Exchange Commission or the Social Security Administration, who decides disputes under the law and regulations administered by his agency, subject to appeals to the Article III courts.

### affidavit
A written statement of facts confirmed by the oath of the party making it, before a notary or officer having authority to administer oaths.

### affirmed
In the practice of the court of appeals, it means that the court of appeals has concluded that the lower court decision is correct and will stand as rendered by the lower court.

### alternative dispute resolution ("ADR")
Methods of resolving a legal dispute without conducting a trial, including mediation and arbitration.

### answer
The formal written statement by a defendant responding to a civil complaint and setting forth the grounds for his or her defense.

### appeal
A request challenging the decision of a trial court by a party that has lost on one or more issues and seeks a higher court (appellate court) review of the decision to determine if it was correct. To make such a request is "to appeal" or "to take an appeal." One who appeals is called the "appellant." The other party is the "appellee."

### arbitration
A form of alternative dispute resolution in which an arbitrator (a neutral decision maker) issues a judgment on the legal issues involved in a case after listening to presentations by each party. Arbitration can be binding or nonbinding, depending on the agreement among the parties before the proceeding.

### arraignment
A proceeding in which an individual who is accused of committing a crime is brought into court, told of the charges, and asked to plead guilty, not guilty, or nolo contendere (no contest).

### Article III judge
A judge who exercises the judicial powers of the United States under the authority of Article III of the U.S. Constitution. Article III judges are appointed by the President, with the advice and consent of the Senate. Article III of the Constitution protects the independence of Article III judges by guaranteeing them a lifetime appointment and no reduction in pay. An Article III judge can only be forcibly removed from office through the impeachment process. Article III judges sit on the U.S. Court of International Trade, the federal district courts, the appeals, and the U.S. Supreme Court.

### bail
Security (usually in the form of money) given for the release of a criminal defendant or witness from legal custody to secure his appearance on the day and time set by the court.

### bankruptcy
A legal process—over which the federal courts have exclusive jurisdiction—by which persons or businesses unable to pay their debts can seek the assistance of the court in liquidating and reorganizing their assets and liabilities. Under the protection of the bankruptcy court, debtors may discharge their debts. Bankruptcy judges preside over these proceedings.

### bankruptcy judge
A federal judge, appointed by the court of appeals for a 14-year term, who has authority to hear matters that arise under the Bankruptcy Code.

### bench trial
Trial by a judge without a jury in which a judge decides which party prevails.

### brief
A written statement submitted by a party in a case that asserts the legal and factual reasons why the party believes the court should decide the case, or particular issues in the case, in that party's favor.

**C**

**capital offense**
A crime punishable by death.

**case law**
The law as reflected in the written decisions of the courts.

**case ancillary to a foreign proceeding**
A case commenced under Chapter 15 of the Bankruptcy Code by the representative of a foreign tribunal to protect the U.S. property of a debtor subject to an insolvency proceeding in another country.

**chambers**
A judge's office, typically including a conference room and work space for the judge's law clerks and secretary.

**chief judge**
The judge who has primary responsibility for the administration of a court. Chief judges are selected from the judges of the court based on seniority.

**circuit executive**
A federal court employee appointed by a circuit judicial council to assist the chief judge of the circuit and provide administrative support to the courts of the circuit.

**clerk of court**
An administrative officer appointed by the judges of the court to manage the flow of cases through the court, maintain court records, handle financial matters, and provide other administrative support to the court.

**common law**
The legal system that originated in England and is in use in the U.S. today. Common law relies on the articulation of legal principles in a historical succession of judicial decisions. Common law principles can be changed by legislation, but legislation is subject to interpretation by common law methodology. Many areas of the law, such as bankruptcy, are now codified in detailed statutes, but these statutes are applied according to their interpretations by successive precedents established by the courts.

**complaint**
A written statement filed by a plaintiff initiating a civil case, stating the jurisdiction of the court to resolve the legal dispute, the wrongs allegedly committed by the defendant, and the requested relief.

**contract**
An agreement between two or more persons that creates an obligation to do or not to do a particular thing.

**conviction**
A judgment of guilt against a criminal defendant.

**counsel**
Legal advice; a term also used to refer to the lawyers in a case.

**court**
Government entity presided over by judges and authorized by statute to resolve legal disputes. Judges sometimes use "court" to refer to themselves in the third person, as in "the court has read the briefs."

**court reporter**
A person who makes a word-for-word record of what is said in court, generally by using a stenographic machine or audio recording, and then produces a transcript of the proceedings upon request.

**Court of International Trade**
A court established by Congress under Article III of the Constitution to hear cases involving U.S. international trade law, including questions concerning tariffs, dumping, countervailing duties, and international property issues.

**damages**
Money paid by defendants to successful plaintiffs in civil cases to compensate the plaintiffs for their injuries.

**debtor**
A person who is the subject of a bankruptcy case.

**default judgment**
A judgment rendered in favor of the plaintiff because of the defendant's failure to answer or appear to contest the plaintiff's claim.

**defendant**
In a civil case, the person or organization against whom the plaintiff brings suit; in a criminal case, the person accused of the crime.

**deposition**
An oral statement made before an officer authorized by law to administer oaths. Such statements are often taken to examine potential witnesses, to obtain discovery, or to be used later in trial.

**discovery**
The process by which lawyers learn about their opponent's case in preparation for trial. Typical tools of discovery include depositions, interrogatories, requests for admissions, and requests for documents. All these devices help the lawyer learn the relevant facts and collect and examine any relevant documents or other materials.

**docket**
A log containing the complete history of each case in the form of brief chronological entries summarizing all court proceedings. All federal court dockets are maintained in electronic form and are generally available to the public by computer.

**en banc**
"In the bench" or "as a full bench." Refers to court sessions with the entire membership of a court participating. U.S. circuit courts of appeals usually decide matters sitting in panels of three judges, but all the judges in the court may decide certain matters together or review panel decisions sitting "en banc" (occasionally spelled "in banc"). The largest courts of appeals may split their full membership into two en banc panels.

**equitable**
Pertaining to civil suits in "equity" rather than in "law." In English legal history, the courts of "law" could order the payment of damages and could afford no other remedy. See "damages." A separate court of "equity" could order someone to do something or to cease to do something. See, e.g., "injunction." In American jurisprudence, the federal courts have both legal and equitable power, but the distinction is still an important one in certain respects. For example, a trial by jury is normally available in cases at "law" but not in "equity."

**evidence**
Physical material or information presented in testimony or in documents that is used to persuade the fact finder (judge or jury) to decide the case in favor of one side or the other. The federal courts must follow the Federal Rules of Evidence.

**federal public defender**
An attorney employed by the federal courts on a full-time basis to provide legal defense to defendants who are unable to afford counsel. The judiciary administers the federal defender program pursuant to the Criminal Justice Act.

**federal question jurisdiction**
Jurisdiction given to federal courts in cases involving the interpretation and application of the U.S. Constitution, acts of Congress, and treaties.

**felony**
A serious crime carrying a penalty of more than one year in prison. Compare with "misdemeanor."

**file**
(1) The act of transmitting or placing a document in the official custody of the clerk of court and entering it into the file or record of a case; (2) the official record of a case.

**grand jury**
A body of 16-23 citizens who listen to evidence of criminal allegations presented by the prosecutors, and determine whether there is enough evidence to issue an indictment and conduct a trial. See also "indictment" and "United States attorney."

**habeas corpus**
A writ (court order) that is usually used to bring a prisoner before the court to determine the legality of his or her imprisonment. Someone in state prison may file a petition in federal court for a "writ of habeas corpus," seeking to have the federal court review whether the state violated his or her rights under the U.S. Constitution. Federal prisoners may file habeas petitions as well. A writ of habeas corpus may also be used to bring a person in custody before the court to give testimony or to be prosecuted.

**hearsay**
Statements by a witness who did not see or hear the incident in question but heard about it second-hand from someone else. Hearsay is usually not admissible as direct evidence in court because it does not allow a defendant to confront his or her accusers and is not as reliable as first-hand testimony, but there are many exceptions to the hearsay rule.

### impeachment
(1) The process of calling a witness's testimony into doubt. For example, if the attorney can show that the witness may have fabricated portions of his testimony, the witness is said to be "impeached." (2) The constitutional process whereby the House of Representatives may "impeach" (accuse of misconduct) high officers of the federal government, who are then removed from office if found guilty in a trial before the Senate.

### indictment
The formal charge issued by a grand jury stating that there is enough evidence that the defendant committed a crime to justify having a trial; it is used primarily for felonies. See also "information."

### in forma pauperis
"In the manner of a pauper." The court may grant a litigant's motion to proceed "in forma pauperis" and allow him or her to file a case without payment of the required court fees if the person does not have the financial means to pay a fee.

### information
A formal accusation by a government attorney that the defendant committed a misdemeanor. An information may also be used in a felony case if the defendant formally waives his or her right to a grand jury indictment. See also "indictment."

### injunction
A court order prohibiting a defendant from performing a specific act, or compelling a defendant to perform a specific act.

### interrogatories
Written questions sent by one party in a lawsuit to an opposing party as part of pretrial discovery in civil cases. The party receiving the interrogatories is required to answer them in writing under oath.

### issue
(1) A disputed point between parties in a lawsuit. (2) To send out officially, as in a court issuing an order.

### judge
An official with statutory authority to decide legal disputes according to the law. Used ge-

nerically, the term "judge" may refer to all judicial officers, including Supreme Court justices, state and federal judges, military judges, and executive branch appointees who preside over tribunals and other bodies that decide legal disputes. See also "Article III judge," "magistrate judge," and "bankruptcy judge."

**judgment**
The official decision of a court finally resolving a dispute between the parties to a lawsuit.

**jurisdiction**
(1) The legal authority or competence of a court to hear and decide a case. (2) The geographic area over which the court has authority to decide cases.

**jurisprudence**
The study of law and the structure of the legal system.

**jury**
The group of local citizens selected by the court to hear the evidence in a trial and render a verdict on matters of fact. See also "grand jury."

**jury instructions**
A judge's directions to the jury before it begins deliberations regarding the factual questions that it must answer and the legal rules that it must apply.

---

**l**

**lawsuit**
A legal action started by a plaintiff against a defendant based on a complaint that the defendant failed to perform a legal duty which resulted in harm to the plaintiff.

**litigation**
A case, controversy, or lawsuit. Participants (plaintiffs and defendants) in lawsuits are called litigants.

---

**magistrate judge**
A federal judge, appointed by a concurrence of a majority of the court's district judges, who conducts initial proceedings in criminal cases, decides criminal misdemeanor cases, conducts many pretrial civil and criminal matters on behalf of district judges, and decides civil cases with the consent of the parties.

**mediation**

The alternative dispute resolution (ADR) method most commonly used in the district courts. Mediation is an informal process in which a mediator facilitates negotiations between the parties to help them resolve their dispute.

**misdemeanor**

An offense punishable by one year of imprisonment or less. Compare with "felony."

**mistrial**

An invalid trial, caused by fundamental error. When a mistrial is declared, the trial must start again with the selection of a new jury.

**motion**

A request by a litigant to a judge for a decision on an issue relating to the case.

**nolo contendere**

No contest. A plea of nolo contendere has the same effect as a plea of guilty, as far as the criminal sentence is concerned, but may not be considered as an admission of guilt for any other purpose.

**opinion**

A judge's written explanation of the decision of the court. Because a case may be heard by three or more judges in the court of appeals, the opinion in appellate decisions can take several forms. If all the judges completely agree on the result, one judge will write the opinion for all. If all the judges do not agree, the formal decision will be based upon the view of the majority, and one member of the majority will write the opinion. The judges who did not agree with the majority may write separately in dissenting or concurring opinions to present their views. A dissenting opinion disagrees with the majority opinion because of the reasoning and/or the principles of law the majority used to decide the case. A concurring opinion agrees with the decision of the majority opinion, but offers further comment or clarification or even an entirely different reason for reaching the same result. Only the majority opinion can serve as binding precedent in future cases. See also "precedent."

**oral argument**

An opportunity for lawyers to verbally summarize their positions before the court and answer the judges' questions.

**p**

**panel**
(1) In appellate cases, a group of judges (usually three) assigned to decide the case. (2) In the jury selection process, the group of potential jurors. (3) The list of attorneys who are both available and qualified to serve as court-appointed counsel for criminal defendants who cannot afford their own counsel.

**party**
One of the litigants in a case. At the trial level, the parties are typically referred to as the plaintiff and defendant. On appeal, they are known as the appellant and appellee, or, in some cases involving administrative agencies, as the petitioner and respondent.

**petit jury (or trial jury)**
A group of citizens who hear the evidence presented by both sides at trial and determine the facts in dispute. Federal criminal juries consist of 12 persons. Federal civil juries consist of at least six persons. See also "jury" and "grand jury."

**petty offense**
A federal misdemeanor punishable by six months or less in prison.

**plaintiff**
The person who initiates a civil lawsuit.

**plea**
In a criminal case, the defendant's statement pleading "guilty," "not guilty," or "no contest" in answer to the charges.

**pleadings**
Written statements filed with the court that describe a party's legal or factual assertions about the case.

**precedent**
A court decision in an earlier case with facts and legal issues similar to a dispute currently before a court. Judges—following the common-law tradition—will generally "follow precedent." They use the principles established in earlier cases to decide new cases that have similar facts and raise similar legal issues. A judge will disregard precedent if a party can show that the earlier case was wrongly decided, or that it differed in some significant way from the current case. Lower courts must follow precedents set by the decisions of higher courts.

**presentence report**
A report prepared by a court's probation officer, after a person has been convicted of an offense, summarizing for the court the background information needed to determine the appropriate sentence.

**pretrial conference**
A meeting of the judge and lawyers to plan the trial, to discuss which matters should be presented to the jury, to review proposed evidence and witnesses, and to set a trial schedule. Typically, the judge and the parties also discuss the possibility of settling of the case.

**pretrial services**
A department of the district court that conducts an investigation of a criminal defendant's background in order to help a judge decide whether to release the defendant into the community before trial.

**probation**
(1) A sentencing alternative to imprisonment in which the court releases convicted defendants under supervision of a probation officer, who makes certain that the defendant follows certain rules (e.g., gets a job, gets drug counseling, etc.) (2) A department of the court that prepares a presentence report in a criminal case.

**probation officer**
Officers of a court who conduct presentence investigations, prepare presentence reports on convicted defendants, and supervise released defendants.

**pro bono publico ("pro bono")**
A Latin term meaning "for the good of the public." Some lawyers take on certain kinds of cases pro bono, without expectation of payment; these cases are called "pro bono cases."

**procedure**
The rules for conducting a lawsuit. There are rules of civil, criminal, bankruptcy, and appellate procedure.

**pro per**
A slang expression sometimes used to refer to a pro se litigant. It is a corruption of the Latin phrase "in propria persona."

**pro se**
A Latin term meaning "on one's own behalf." In courts, it refers to persons who present their own cases without lawyers.

**prosecute**
To charge someone with a crime. A prosecutor tries a criminal case on behalf of the gov-ernment.

---

 **recalled judge**
A retired magistrate judge, bankruptcy judge, or judge of the Court of Federal Claims may return to duty for a limited term as a "recalled" judge.

**record**
A written account of the proceedings in a case, including all pleadings, evidence, and exhib-its submitted in the course of the case.

**remand**
The act of an appellate court sending a case to a lower court for further proceedings.

**reverse**
The act of an appellate court setting aside the decision of a trial court. A reversal is often accompanied by a remand to the lower court for further proceedings.

---

**senior judge**
An Article III judge who has retired from active duty but continues to perform some judicial duties, usually maintaining a reduced caseload. Commonly referred to as "senior status." A judge who has not taken senior status may be referred to as an "active judge," although the distinction may be misleading as many senior judges maintain full caseloads.

**sentence**
The punishment ordered by a court for a defendant convicted of a crime.

**sentencing guidelines**
A set of rules and principles established by the United States Sentencing Commission that trial judges use as one factor to consider when they determine the sentence for a convicted defendant.

**sequester**
To separate. Sometimes juries are sequestered or isolated from outside influences during their deliberations.

**service of process**
The delivery of writs or summonses to a party in a lawsuit or someone involved in the case.

**settlement**
Parties to a lawsuit resolve their dispute without having a trial. Settlements often involve the payment of compensation by one party in at least partial satisfaction of the other party's claims, but usually do not include the admission of fault.

**statute**
A law passed by a legislature.

**statute of limitations**
A law that sets the deadline by which parties must file suit to enforce their rights. For example, if a state has a five-year statute of limitations for breaches of contract, and John breached a contract with Susan on January 1, 2005, Susan must file her lawsuit by January 1, 2010. If the deadline passes, the "statute of limitations has run" and the party may be prohibited from bringing a lawsuit; i.e., the claim is "time-barred." Sometimes a party's attempt to assert his or her rights will "toll" the statute of limitations, giving the party additional time to file suit.

**subpoena**
A command, issued under authority of a court or other authorized government entity, to compel an individual or organization to produce some kind of evidence, or require a witness to appear and give testimony.

**subpoena duces tecum**
A command to a witness to appear and produce documents.

**summary judgment**
A decision made on the basis of statements and evidence presented for the record without a trial. It is used when it is not necessary to resolve any factual disputes in the case. Summary judgment is granted when—on the undisputed facts in the record—one party is entitled to judgment as a matter of law.

**temporary restraining order**
Prohibits a person from taking an action that is likely to cause irreparable harm. This differs from an injunction in that it may be granted immediately, without notice to the opposing party, and without a hearing. It is intended to last only until a hearing can be held. Sometimes referred to as a "T.R.O."

**testimony**

Evidence presented orally by witnesses during trials or before grand juries.

**toll**

See "statute of limitations." Certain actions will "toll" the statute of limitations, or extend the time by which parties must file suit to enforce their rights.

**tort**

A civil wrong or breach of a duty to another person. The "victim" of a tort may be entitled to sue for the harm suffered. Victims of crimes may also sue in tort for the wrongs done to them. Most tort cases are handled in state court, except when the tort occurs on federal property (e.g., a military base), when the government is the defendant, or when a dispute between parties from different states falls under the federal court's diversity jurisdiction.

**transcript**

A written, word-for-word record of what was said, either in a proceeding such as a trial, or during some other formal conversation, such as a hearing or oral deposition.

**trustee**

In a bankruptcy case, a person appointed to represent the interests of the bankruptcy estate and the unsecured creditors. The trustee's responsibilities may include liquidating the prop-erty of the estate, making distributions to creditors, and bringing actions against creditors or the debtor to recover property of the bankruptcy estate.

---

 **uphold**

The appellate court agrees with the lower court decision and allows it to stand. See "af-firmed."

**U.S. attorney**

A lawyer appointed by the President of the United States in each judicial district to prose-cute and defend cases for the federal government. The U.S. attorney employs a staff of as-sistant U.S. attorneys (AUSAs) who appear as the government's attorneys in individual cases.

**U.S. trustee**

The United States Trustee Program is a component of the United States Department of Jus-tice responsible for overseeing the administration of bankruptcy cases and private trustees. United States Trustees are government employees appointed by the Attorney General of the United States. United States Trustees appoint and supervise private trustees, take legal action to enforce the requirements of the United States Bankruptcy Code, refer matters for investigation and criminal prosecution, and ensure that bankruptcy estates are administered efficiently and that professional fees are reasonable.

### venue
The geographical location in which a case is tried.

### verdict
The decision of a trial jury or a judge that determines the guilt or innocence of a criminal defendant, or that determines the final outcome of a civil case.

### voir dire
The process by which judges and lawyers select a trial jury from among those eligible to serve by questioning them to make certain that they would fairly decide the case. "Voir dire" is a phrase meaning "to speak the truth."

### warrant
An arrest warrant is a written court order authorizing official action by law enforcement officials, usually directing them to arrest the individual named in the warrant. A search warrant is a court order that permits a specific location be searched for items which, if found, can be used in court as evidence.

### witness
A person called upon by either side in a lawsuit to give testimony before the court or jury.

### writ
A formal written command or order, issued by the court, requiring the performance of a specific act.

### writ of certiorari
An order issued by the U.S. Supreme Court directing the lower court to transmit records for a case it will hear on appeal. ∎

# ABOUT THE ADMINISTRATIVE OFFICE OF THE UNITED STATES COURTS

Created by an Act of Congress in 1939, the Administrative Office of the U.S. Courts supports the work of the judicial branch. Its Director, who serves as the chief administrative officer for the federal courts, is appointed by the Chief Justice of the United States in consultation with the Judicial Conference of the United States.

The Administrative Office provides staff support and counsel to the judiciary's policymaking body, the Judicial Conference of the United States, and its committees. It monitors and assesses judiciary operations and emerging issues, makes recommendations for new policies and programs, and implements and promotes the Judicial Conference's policies.

The Administrative Office develops programs, systems, and methods to support and improve judicial administration. It provides a broad array of administrative, legal, technical, communications, and other services that support the operation of the federal appellate, district, and bankruptcy courts, and the defender services and probation and pretrial services programs. Among its many functions, the Administrative Office develops and administers the judiciary's budget; audits court financial records; manages the judiciary's payroll and human resources programs; collects and analyzes statistics to report on the business of the courts; manages the judiciary's automation and information technology programs;

conducts studies and reviews of programs and operations; develops new business methods for the courts; provides training and technical assistance; issues manuals, directives, rules, and other publications; fosters and coordinates communications with the legislative and executive branches; and provides public information.

The Administrative Office's Director has delegated to the individual courts many of his statutory administrative authorities. As a result, each court can plan, organize, and manage its business activities and expenditures, consistent with policies and spending limits, to meet its particular needs. This decentralization of administrative authority benefits both the courts and the taxpayers because it reduces bureaucracy and encourages innovation and economy. ∎

## SOURCES OF ADDITIONAL INFORMATION

### Publications
Federal Courts and What They Do
(Federal Judicial Center, 2006)

Strategic Plan for the Federal Judiciary
(Judicial Conference of the United States, 2010)

### Judiciary Website Addresses
Administrative Office of the U.S. Courts
www.uscourts.gov

### Federal Judicial Center
www.fjc.gov

### Authorized Judgeships
For current information on authorized federal judgeships visit the judges and judgeships section of www.uscourts.gov

www.ingramcontent.com/pod-product-compliance
Lightning Source LLC
Chambersburg PA
CBHW080608190526
45169CB00007B/2926